ELISHA
&
The Tale of Two Weddings

Benjamin Sabaroche

Illustrated by Chieze Ihecherenoma

Copyright © 2019 Benjamin Sabaroche. All rights reserved.
First paperback edition printed 2019 in the
United Kingdom
A catalogue record for this book is available from
the British Library.
ISBN 978-1-913455-06-4
No part of this book shall be reproduced or transmitted in
any form or by any means,
electronic or mechanical, including photocopying,
recording, or by any information retrieval
system without written permission of the publisher.
Published by Scribblecity Publications
Printed in Great Britain
Although every precaution has been taken in the
preparation of this book, the publisher and
author assume no responsibility for errors or omissions.
Neither is any liability assumed for
damages resulting from the use of this information
contained herein.

Hello, My name is Elisha, I am 8 years old and I live with my mum, dad and little sister Amara.

I love to write about my amazing, astonishing life and this is the tale of the two weddings!

BIG NEWS

My mum told me some exciting news! Her sister, my auntie Mary is getting married. I'm going to have a new uncle, and his name is Joe.

Everybody is so happy especially my Grandma. She was on the phone to everyone.

I call her Grandma Cakes, as she bakes the most mouth-watering cakes every time she visits.

BLAH BLAH BLAH YES OOH!

TWO OUTFITS?

I haven't been to a wedding before.

"I'm going to look good in my shiny new suit", I told grandma.

Grandma Cakes explained , "We have so much to plan and do". "Elisha, you and your sister will look lovely in your African clothes!"

I was stunned.

"Grandma, I thought I was going to wear a suit?"

GRANDMA EXPLAINS

As she sat next to me, she explained.

"Well Elisha, in our culture we have 2 weddings. The traditional African wedding is how the two families come together and celebrate. We wear colourful African clothing, eat our favourite foods and have a party. The church wedding is almost the same, but you get to wear a suit."

I smiled a **BIG** smile and said, "So two weddings means two parties! This is so **cool!**"

THE CLOTHES (1)

"Grandma, where do we buy the traditional clothes?", I asked.

"We don't buy the clothes, Elisha, we will get them made for us." said Grandma. I was puzzled. She continued.

"Firstly, we go to a special fabric shop to buy the material. There will be so many colours to choose from. Auntie Mary & Uncle Joe have picked their wedding colours for everyone in the family to wear."

I quizzed Grandma, "So I have to wear the same colour as Amara, even if it's pink?!"

Grandma laughed. "No, the bridesmaids will wear blue, the groomsmen, will wear red and the two families will wear green. The colours and styles are so vibrant – the whole day will be **spectacular**!"

THE CLOTHES (2)

Mum showed me the style that I was going to wear. It was a long shirt with short sleeves and trousers. I was going to be wearing green. Oh yeah that is my favourite colour! Mum was going to be wearing blue as she was one of bridesmaids.

Grandma took me to visit the tailor. He worked in a very busy shop, with lots of people around. There were lots of pictures on the wall of people in different African outfits.

He took lots of different measurements
so he could make the clothes fit
me perfectly.

THE CLOTHES (3)

I went shopping again for my suit for the white wedding with my family.
We went to lots of shops and I found a black suit that had a starry space lining!
I loved it and we bought it.

My sister Amara, also needed a white dress. She looked cute in her dress too!

THE TRADITIONAL WEDDING (1)

It was the day of the traditional wedding. Everyone was getting ready for the long and busy day.

My mum was helping grandma cooking the food. The lovely smell of Jollof rice filled the air – **mmm**, delicious! My mum said that I could help film the day, so she helped me set up the camera to record everything.

Everyone had helped get the hall ready. There was so much to see – drinks on the table, the **lovely decorations, the balloons and the phenomenal FOOD!**

Jollof rice, plantain, fried rice, chicken, fish, egusi soup, puff-puff and my favourite snack – **chin-chin! Yum, yum!!**

THE TRADITIONAL WEDDING (2)

I was looking incredible in my new African clothes.

The bride and groom's mums came in first singing and dancing a traditional igbo gospel song with some of their friends.

The bridesmaids and groomsmen all had to dance into the hall.

My Auntie Mary & Uncle Joe were wearing dazzling purple outfits. They looked like an African King & Queen, and they had to dance into the hall too.
I filmed the whole thing!

I sat on a special table with Grandma, Dad and Amara. Mum was looking after Auntie Mary and making sure everything was fine.

TRADITIONAL WEDDING

When everyone had sat down, brought in what they called **Kola-nut** in a tray and it was time for breaking Kola-nut.

I asked grandma why the Kola-nut? She explained to me that it was an **Igbo** tradition that symbolises hospitality, friendship and respect.

The Traditional Wedding (3)

My belly roared. I asked Grandma, "I'm hungry and the **Jollof rice** looks so **tasty**."

Grandma said, "We can eat after this dance."

Auntie Mary & Uncle Joe were dancing and people were coming and putting money on their heads.

"Why are people putting money on them?" I asked excitedly.

Grandma replied, "Elisha, this is a special tradition for people to give money to the couple to start their new life."

"Ok. So can I have the money dance on my birthday? "I asked Grandma and flashed a big grin.

Grandma laughed, "Sorry Elisha, you have to wait until you get married!"

Grandma, Amara, Mum and me helped pick up all the money while they were dancing.

Afterwards, we ate the delicious food and danced into the night, until I fell asleep. I was **SOOOO** tired!

The White Wedding (1)

When it was time for the white wedding, Mum told me that we would have a special treat. We would be staying in a hotel!

I was **super** excited!
We packed our bags with all the clothes for the wedding and off we went.

The hotel was a really tall building. I would be staying in a room with Grandma and Amara. Mum would stay with Auntie Mary.

In the morning, we had to get up really early. We went to have breakfast in the hotel restaurant.

There was so much **food!**

"Mum, what can I have to eat?", I asked.

"Honey, it's going to be a long day and you can have cereal first and anything else you want afterwards." said Mum

I was so **happy!** I ate lots of croissants and toast!

The White Wedding (2)

After breakfast, we got dressed and waited with Grandma for Auntie Mary.

She was having pictures taken and being filmed as she was getting ready. Mum was helping her, and they both looked fantastic.

When it was time to go, Grandma and Auntie Mary went in a special car with white ribbons.

The second wedding was in a big hall that was very old called Alexandra Palace, even older than Grandma!

The White Wedding (3)

I had to walk down the aisle with Amara. She didn't want to. Mum had to promise her a treat if she did. So **annoying!** We walked down the aisle and then sat next to Grandma.

After the wedding, we went outside to the gardens to take pictures. It was a scorching sunny day and as we walked back, there was an ice cream van. Mum bought us a lolly each to cool down.

The White Wedding (4)

At the wedding reception, Auntie Mary & Uncle Joe had arranged lots of food, including my favourite, mini burgers! **Yummy!**

After dinner, Auntie Mary and Uncle Joe cut an enormous cake. There were 4 cakes on top of each other! The cake was very tasty.

The day finished with everyone dancing and Amara was quiet!
She was sleeping on Mummy's lap!

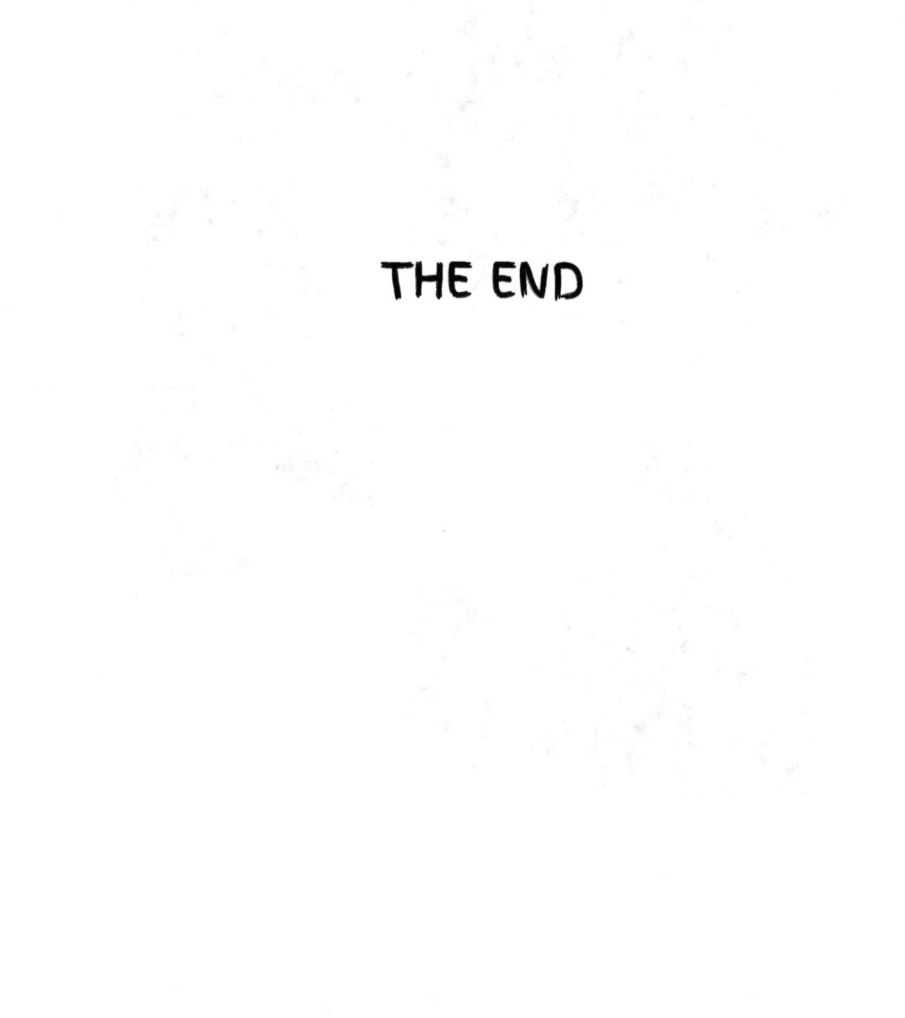

www.ingramcontent.com/pod-product-compliance
Lightning Source LLC
Chambersburg PA
CBHW071508080526
44587CB00016B/2729